Charged With A Crime In Texas?

Useful Info That May Help You In Your Case

Bobby Dale Barina, Esq.

ISBN: 978-1-941645-49-9

Designed and Published by:

Speakeasy Publications

73-03 Bell Blvd #10

Oakland Gardens, NY 11364

888-225-8594

www.SpeakeasyMarketingInc.com

DISCLAIMER

This publication is intended to be informational only. The information in this book is not intended as legal advice. No legal advice is being given, and no attorney-client relationship is intended to be created by reading this material. If you are facing legal issues, whether criminal or civil, seek professional legal counsel to get your questions answered.

Bobby Dale Barina,

455 E. Central Texas Expy

Suite 104

Harker Heights, TX 76548

(254) 870-9947

www.BobbyDaleBarina.com

TESTIMONIALS

"I can say my world was turned upside down, and never thought I would need the assistance of an attorney. While conducting a Google search, I found Bobby Dale Barina. After reading their home page, my gut said go with them, and I'm glad I did. They are very professional and gave me great advice along the way. When I thought that all hope was gone, the expert advice of the talented lawyers and staff helped me every step of the way. I was never kept in the dark, and was always advised of the steps I needed to take. My case was later dismissed and I was able to work on getting my life back together. I highly recommend these professionals to anyone in need of a great defense attorney." ***- A Former Client***

"We are really happy and satisfied with their service. The outcome of the case made them even more inordinate in our eyes as we won the case without having any kind of further problems. The attorney really helped us even though he was busy in his schedule. Really want to thank you for your service and effort made on our case." ***- Shannon T.***

"He fought for me when I was accused of a crime. Every other lawyer told me to plead out, but not him. He listened to what I wanted and he helped me." ***- Ronald***

"On the worst day of your life, you want this guy. Bobby Barina has been the attorney for my family for many years now. No matter how busy he is, he always makes you feel like you are the only client he has." ***- Brandon H.***

TABLE OF CONTENTS

AUTHOR INTRODUCTION

I'm board certified in both family law and criminal law, and I've tried cases in every area of my practice. While there are many Texas lawyers who can boast of experience, what sets my firm apart is personal service. Personally handling every case that comes into my office, I'll prepare your case from the opening.

My areas of practice include

- Family Law
- Criminal Law
- Custody & Visitation
- DUI/DWI
- Divorce
- Adoption
- Child Support

1. Types of Cases That We Handle

We handle many types of cases here. Fort Hood, the largest military base in the free world, is located here. I have been practicing criminal law for 24 years. I went to work right out of law school for a board-certified criminal defense lawyer and that's really what I started doing. I have been a prosecutor as well as a special prosecutor in Coryell County. I've tried every kind of case you could imagine. I've also been a prosecutor in Bell County, Texas and a chief juvenile prosecutor, so I've handled a lot of things. From the screening process to the presentation of cases to the jury, to the judge, and to grand juries, I've handled literally thousands of cases over the last 24 years.

How do you think your background as a prosecutor plays into how you handle criminal defense? I would think it gives you a leg up.

It really does. It allows you to see the process from both sides. It allows you to see how statements are taken, how evidence is taken, and how judges really receive the information. When you're a prosecutor, the only thing you're focused on is what you're doing for the office in front of the judge. It gives you the ability to really figure out how they receive the information and what the weak points are in your case, or how officers traditionally do things, or the training materials. It gives you a whole wealth of information that you would not have otherwise.

I also think if you've been practicing in the same area for some time, you develop some relationships with the prosecutors and the judges.

Everybody is different. Every judge likes to do things differently in their own unique way, and so do prosecutors. You get to know who they are just by talking to them or even being in their office. Their offices are decorated with the things that they are proud of, or there are books on the shelves that they refer to from time to time, and pictures of their families and vacation spots, and everything you take in is important.

Once I was in a judge's office when we had a difference of opinion about a jury charge issue, and he reached up and picked up a book from his bookshelf that was an obscure title in those days.

I went out and bought that book the very first day because I knew that's the one he relied on. I would have never known that unless I was in his office. So after that, when I wanted to tell that judge something, I could tell him the page that he could find it on in that book, and it really helped me understand what he wanted to see based on the text and the comment notes at the bottom of the page.

Does that give you a little insight into who you're dealing with?

Yes. That's really what we do as lawyers. Information is the best thing. If I am representing somebody, I want to go and see them. I want to know who they are. I want to see what pictures they have on their walls. I want to see how they prepare their own home. Where do people interact? Where do they sit? Are they kitchen people or are they living room people? How social are they? I can tell this by looking at how they arrange themselves and their house. Where have they been? How do they think? What are they proud of?

It's the same thing as dealing with a professional. If I have an expert who is going to testify in a case, particularly if he's going to testify for the other side, I don't want to meet with him outside, and I don't want to meet with him in the lobby; I want to meet with him in his office. You'll see some of the older prosecutors refuse to meet with some people in their office because they don't want to give away much information about who they are and where they come from.

You can even pick up a lot from looking at their walls and seeing where they went to school, particularly if it's a situation where you're in the same timeframe within 5 or 6 years either way from when they started or when they finished law school. You know who they learned from and how they processed that information.

2. Types of Criminal Defense Cases That We Handle

When you get down to the bread and butter or the meat and potatoes of it, the cases that recur over and over and over are unfortunately DWIs or DUIs. DUI in Texas is driving under the influence, and that's 21 years of age or less. If they have any detectable alcohol in their system, then they can be charged with DUI. If they're over that age, then they would have to have a blood alcohol level of 0.08 or the loss of the normal use of their mental and physical faculties. Those are the bigger cases. Possession of marijuana (you see those cases in the misdemeanor courts constantly), domestic violence, and assault cases are really the biggest ones on the misdemeanor side.

When you get into the felony side, it's possession of a controlled substance, whatever that might be in that timeframe. Sometimes, a meth crisis will go on for years, meaning methamphetamine or crystal meth, and then it'll be cocaine or heroin, if they're making a comeback, in which case it's easier to make and distribute those things. Those are the cases you see most often.

Do you also represent military clients often? What kinds of services do you offer them being so close to the base?

Well, they have a number of concerns. When you're subject to the uniform code of military justice, you can also be tried in the military courts, and that's an entirely different process that involves dealing with the articles. There's Article 15, involving the things you keep in house or in your company, and in your take and command, all the way to Article 32, a hearing for probable cause for a general court-martial. We're always trying to keep our eyes on how anything we do in this case is going to affect them. Right now, we're dealing with the downturn and downsizing of the American military.

So you have a lot of people who would be separated just basically on the accusation of a case. If it's a case of domestic violence or a case that's a misunderstanding, what we try to do then is to move as quickly as possible to get investigators in there to get some statements taken, so we can turn to their chain of command to say, "This is being taken care of," or, "This isn't somebody you need to separate from his military obligations based on the accusation." Then we talk about counseling and getting them into something that we know the American military complex is really keen on. If it's something to do with sexual harassment, another sexual crime, or even a misunderstanding, we make sure that we get that person into counseling as soon as possible so we alleviate concerns about how they talk to individuals.

3. Misconceptions People Have When Arrested in Texas

People have the misconception of what lawyers do for living. The biggest misconception is that if they're innocent, they are going to be able to convince the police of this. They're going to want to talk to the police and convince them that this is not a problem, that this has never happened, and that they are not responsible for this crime. Some people believe that they can offer up an explanation or an excuse for their actions and people will believe that, and they can get past it. In our everyday life, if we apologize and we say we were wrong, people will generally say, "Okay, that's fine." That even goes for political figures. Say “I've done wrong” and “I'm sorry,” and everything goes away.

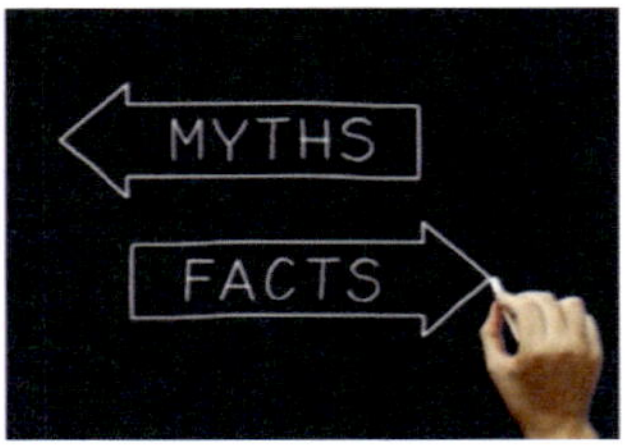

That's not how it works in the criminal justice system. They want to know what you did if you did it, and where to go from there as far as punishment. When they deal with us, their misconception is that we are somehow part of this process that's there to incarcerate them. Some people have to deal with public defenders or court-appointed attorneys, and they believe that these people are part of that process. They want to just get along with the prosecutors and the judges. That's a giant misconception: that they're not going to try hard, that they're going to talk you and ask you to plead guilty.

The majority of people who practice court-appointed work are really there to do best job they can. But it's a misconception we have a hard time getting away from when educating the general public.

What have you learned about people's behavior and their reaction to being arrested and prosecuted for crimes?

Everybody has a different reaction. All people are different. You go to some people when they are arrested for a crime and they're shocked. Some are confused, some of them are mad, and some of them are hurt. Everybody reacts a little bit differently to it.

The one thing that I would say that most people have in common is that when they are arrested for a crime, they want to talk about it. At the same time, they don't want anybody else to talk about it and they don't want anybody to know what they're going through, because obviously there's a stigma in being associated with a crime. Still, they want to talk about it at the same time. So as much as we tell them, "Hey, you have a right to remain silent," and then, tongue in cheek, "You need to use it," it's not going to happen. They are going to say something to somebody.

What are Miranda Rights and when do they actually come into play? What are some of the misconceptions there?

There are a lot of misconceptions about Miranda Rights. It is the right to remain silent when you're: 1) in custody, and 2) you're subject to questioning. Now, there are also some limited exceptions to that. If you're the one person who is the source of the investigation, then maybe you're not in custody, but there is still questioning. Someone might say, "Well, he didn't read me my Miranda Rights." My question then would be, “Did he ask you any questions at all?” If not, then he just arrested you with a warrant and because there is no questioning going on, they don’t need to talk to you about your right to remain silent because it's not relevant. Any time you come into contact with the police or confront them when they’re asking you questions, though, be it on the roadside or at home, you have the right to simply say "I don’t wish to speak to you" or keep quiet.

Now, it's always easier to tell them who you are and things like that, but any time you're being subjected to questions by the police, you have that right to remain silent. That's just a fundamental right that we have in our constitution, but it comes into play during that questioning.

I've heard people say, especially in DUI cases, "Well, they didn't read me my Miranda Rights, so this case is going to be thrown out." Can you elaborate on that?

Yes. DWI cases are one of those rare situations, even though they happen all the time, where you have to think about what a DWI is saying. We're telling the world that this one individual has consumed alcohol or another substance to the point where they lost the normal use of their mental and physical faculties. So the police will ask some general questions only to determine who you are and to try to get a feel for safety. For instance, "Where are you going? What's your name? Do you have insurance? Do you have a driver's license?" When they are asking those questions, they are also there to record your answers so that a jury can listen to the way you speak later. Then if you testify in court, they can draw the distinction about whether or not you lost the normal use of your mental and physical faculties.

So no case is ever just thrown out. The defendant can file a motion to suppress the evidence obtained by the police as a result of improper questioning in violation of Miranda, but it doesn't just throw out the case. They can still proceed with their other evidence and they can even appeal a judge's decision if it's prior to trial.

Do you ever have clients who feel guilty or know they're guilty and think they can just plead guilty and throw themselves on the mercy of the court? If so, what do you tell them?

Yes, that happens a lot honestly. They believe they're guilty and they want to get this over with as quickly as possible. Those individuals come to that point for a variety of reasons, but their expectation is, "It will result in a better outcome for me if I just tell them I did it." In these cases, you're dealing with law enforcement officers and the prosecutor's office, and they have a lot to do. They have a lot of cases pending and the population goes up all the time. If you want to go ahead and say you did it, you are not going to be rewarded with a lighter punishment. In fact, it will probably be worse because they don't have to worry about your case. You already told them that you're going to work it out with them no matter what. So I always give people the same advice: Why do we need to go down that particular road right now? Let's find out what they're saying, let's find out who said what, let's get a better grasp of the discovery, and let's talk to them. Let's see what they want to do as far as working this case out, and what our options are.

You really have to spend some time going back and forth while the client comes in and says, "I want to get this over as quickly as possible." Well, okay, great. It's going to take a number of weeks for the file to be set up at the local prosecutor's office. If they are in jail, it comes a little bit quicker. Do we need a grand jury indictment? For a felony, we do; for a misdemeanor, we don’t. How long is that going to take? Is it drug-related? If it is, then the lab has to test the samples — and I'm talking about controlled substances here – and then come back. We can't just run over there and expect them to know everything about the case immediately.

Now, there are some cases where people are caught in a violent act and they remain incarcerated for a period of time, and the prosecutors know 90% of what they're ever going to know about the case. But let's still be clear. Let's take it one step at a time and find out as much as possible, because throwing yourself on the mercy of the court is never the best outcome. You want to find out what it is, you want to talk about it, and you want to see what can be done to mitigate that punishment. Somebody who says "I was in possession of the controlled substance, so I'm automatically guilty" might not be aware that there are things that we can do. Are you going to NA (Narcotics Anonymous)? Are you seeking to relieve that stress by seeking counseling? If it's something you're self-medicating on, let's make an effort at becoming a better citizen and returning to public life immediately, rather than just running over there and telling them, "Throw me in prison," if that's what you're going to do.

4. Chances of Your Arrest Being Public if Charged with a Crime in Texas

It all really depends on what type of case it is. For instance, the DWIs we've been talking about go on your driving record. If part of your job is to drive a vehicle or a truck for the company, the insurance company is going to want to know about a DWI arrest. Some places keep track of how people operate those vehicles and how they drive even when they're not at work. So your work will find out if part of what you do for them is drive.

If it's a regular misdemeanor case, it's rare that everybody's going to find out unless it's a work-related issue. If you're in the military, those guys read the blotter, the arrests, and the detentions that come out from local law enforcement every day. Most people don't hear about cases because they are not publicized, though. Once you get to court, there are so many people in the hallways, but the only people in the courtroom are the people taking care of their case. They don't have enough time and energy to worry about somebody else's case. Your friends and family will usually find out if the defendant has told them. If it's a first degree felony or something unique like a murder case

or a case where a child is kidnapped or anything dramatic that just shocks you to hear about, then that might be played out in the media. That results in everybody in the local community learning about it if they pay attention to the news.

What about an arrest relating to a sex crime charge? Is that going to be a little bit more public?

Generally, if a sex crime case goes to jury trial — and they usually do — then it'll be reported on. Generally, though, cases are pled out or resolved prior to trial. If that happens, then it's usually just a note in the paper that the judge gave somebody a sentence or approved a plea bargain for a sentence. Sometimes that has the defendant's name but not often. It just surprises so many people that sex crimes are cases that go to court all the time. So they are generally not reported on specifically because they're just one of many types of cases.

If you have to register on the sex offender list, then obviously notifications go out, correct?

Well, the notifications go out but they don't go out very far, to a lot of the people and then to the community. If it's related to somebody who is of school age, it goes to teachers and administrators and the school district for the protection of the people around them. But people really don't pay a whole lot of attention to those notifications. When you get on the website or you use a local mobile app that looks for sex offenders in that area, people really become surprised. Every time somebody uses it, they say the same thing: "Wow, I didn't know that this person is living over there." There's just so much information that goes on around this. There is always a chance that it'll go public but it doesn't usually become that public. Some people will find out but it's not just overwhelming to the point where everybody is going to know.

5. Effect of Someone's Background on Criminal Charges in Texas

Well, it's not necessarily the judge, first of all. It's how law enforcement officers deal with you, how the prosecutors deal with you, and then, ultimately, if we get to that point, it's how the judge deals with you.

Let's say you're a good person and you have a family and a good job and, other than this one infraction, you're an upstanding citizen. It matters a great deal.

Now, there is a big difference between a good person and a person who comes from a good family. You being a good person in and of yourself is more important than whether you come from a good family. What does it mean to be a good person? It means something different to everyone. How do we determine that? Where do you go to church? Where did you go to school? Are you involved in activities that benefit others? Are you simply a person who you says you're a good person because you go to work 40 hours a week, you go home, you go to your kid's soccer game, and things of that nature? Or do you do Habitat for Humanity? Do you coach your kid's soccer team? There is a lot that plays into what a good person is based on everybody's

different beliefs about what that means, and it’s measured against others they've known and measured against themselves.

So that's the first part we look at. We ask, "Why do you think you're a good person? You obviously do, so let's hash it out a little bit." That's part of the interview process.

Now, if the client has never been in trouble before, that's in large part because part of the decision for law enforcement about whether or not to file charges is what level of charges to file. It's easier to go down on a case once we start it than to go up. Sometimes law enforcement starts with a higher charge that they believe is possible. Well, if you've never been in trouble before, when you talk to them, you say you were never in trouble before and you didn't know it was drugs. It's not like the average person is going to know what every drug looks like, but if you've been in trouble before, and particularly if you were arrested for drug possession or drug dealing, you're absolutely going to know what the drugs look like, so they're not going to believe you.

When they're looking at your file, the prosecutor will look for felony charges and not at the misdemeanors. They're looking at your criminal history. Now, they don’t know you're a good person at that time unless they know you personally, and so we really have to deal with prior history at that point. Part of the defense lawyer's job is to get in there quickly and paint a better picture of the defendant by pointing out why he is a good person and having that conversation.

If you ever get to the judge, if you've never been in trouble before, then you have a lot more options legally. Is probation or deferred adjudication an option? These things give the court more leeway. For instance, in Texas, we have state jail felonies for possession of certain controlled substances under a gram, and the sentence is probation. That's the first punishment if you've never been in trouble before, because we don't want to lock you up necessarily; we just want to make sure it never happens again, if possible. Regarding possible punishment, if the judge looks at you and you've had one minor scrape with the law or you've never been in trouble before, the court is more likely to believe your story about why this is something you can put behind you. If you're a good person with no criminal history, then that does affect the outcome.

6. Right Time to Contact an Attorney After Being Arrested

There are a few ways to know that you are under criminal investigation and going to be charged with a crime and arrested.

People will tell you, "They're talking to me about you," or, "Somebody asked me questions about you," or, "Somebody from law enforcement contacted your employer," and things like that. If it's a financial case, usually the bank is the first one to tell you, because if they get a subpoena for your bank records, they'll send a copy to you and say, "Hey, we got this thing. They are asking for your records. What do you think about that?" Generally when they come and see me at that point, I say, "Well, they're going to get them one way or another," and then we go from there. So you just notice things around you like people talking about you and asking questions about you, and then it moves up a little bit. It depends on what sort of investigation it is. Again, for financial crimes, they always start at a distance, and move in towards what they believe the target is. One of their goals is to talk to the accused, and the next goal is successful prosecution, but you're really just hearing things.

What is your recommendation in terms of when you should get an attorney involved? What do you say to people who are nervous to get an attorney involved because they know they're guilty?

It never helps. The police are not there to see your point of view. Like every person alive, they have their own preconceptions, and sometimes those conceptions are misconceptions, but they are not there just for you to go down and tell them, "Hey, I didn't do it." They may believe you or they may not, but you should always have an attorney present any time you're speaking to someone from law enforcement because that person gives you a buffer, a sounding board, and the ability to say, "We're done. I'm going to get up and walk away." In addition, when the police are misleading somebody in an effort to get more information, the lawyer will know it, and they can get up and say, "Okay, we're done," or, "This interview is over." So don't ever just voluntarily jump up and say, "I'm going down to talk to the police officer about myself." It is not wise. It never helps.

So hiring a lawyer isn't going to harm your case any further. It's not like they're going to say, "Well, he got a lawyer. Let's arrest him now, since he must be guilty."

Well, they might say, "Let's arrest him now." If they have a case they are looking to close and you tell them, "I'd like to hire an attorney," then most officers will say, "Well, if that's the case, you don't need to come in. We're going to file a request for a warrant for your arrest." They've already made that decision.

The only reason they're getting your statement is to lock you in at that point. When they say that, then obviously you know they'd already made up their mind. What if you had already given a statement? You're stuck to that statement. Remember: they're not going to give you a copy of the statement. They'll string you along a little bit by saying, "Okay, let's go back a week." Their story really didn't make sense. It could have happened somewhere else some other way and you're trying to help. Sure, it could have, but now you've given a statement that doesn't have their questions in it and it says, "Well, it happened a different way." Now you look like you're lying and it prevents you from testifying in your own defense because you have inconsistent statements.

These law enforcement people are just like your lawyer. Your lawyer went to law school and studied how evidence is supposed to be presented. The police officer studied how evidence is to be gathered, and they take courses on it all the time. They learn how to take a statement and how to get the best statement. So when you tell them something, it's not going to be something that's favorable to you except under the rarest of circumstances. That's usually when a police officer calls a lawyer and says, "Hey, you know me. I just need to clear this one thing. I've got one specific question." There is a long relationship that's been built up over the years of hearing about this officer and seeing if the conduct has worked. The officer is also saying the same thing about the lawyer. The police officer will think, "This guy is representing this client. He is going to let me talk to him because he knows I am not going to do something to jeopardize our relationship."

Are police actually allowed to lie to you during an interrogation?

Absolutely! It's encouraged. They will lie to you about the facts of the case and the evidence. Now, remember: when they're lying to you, they believe you're guilty, and so that's encouraged to get evidence of you being guilty. Well, she's told us that you did this, or that she saw you, or that you told her at some point. But these things don't have to be true. Police officers, case law, and judges' decisions when people are trying to get this thing thrown out later all say, "No, that's something you

can talk to the jury about, but that's no reason to keep the statement from being included."

In that case, are you allowed to lie to the police?

No. If you give a false statement to a police officer, you're in trouble. Now, interestingly enough, if a police officer gives a false statement to another law enforcement organization – even his own organization – or person, that's something that's frowned upon and illegal as well. It's a one-way street.

7. Indictments and Grand Juries in Texas

When we are talking about indictment, we're talking about grand juries, and these are not juries that are deciding guilt and innocence. Our constitution calls them by the term “grand jury.” If you are asked to answer a felony charge and possibly be incarcerated, you have the right to a grand jury. That’s when we are talking about civilians. If it's a military case, you'd have an Article 32 hearing for the determination of probable cause. And that's what a grand jury does. In our area, 12 people come in and they listen to the evidence, and that evidence can be announced to them, they can be shown it, there can be witnesses, or they can just have a prosecutor say, "I've read in this report that this was said." Then what they're asked to do is vote on whether it’s a true bill or not a true bill. If 9 people say there is a true bill, then what the grand jury has determined is that there is probable cause to believe an offense has been committed.

Probable cause is a really weird concept. It's just a reasonable belief that a crime was committed by the individual who's been accused of it. If there is probable cause to believe that this crime was committed at the location that they are talking about, and if this location had the evidence, then it's probable cause to believe. That's just kind of a weird statement. They're just trying to say, "We don't want a prosecutor to be able just to go to court based on a whim." They have to have a buffer, and that buffer is the grand jury.

So it's a system of checks and balances where the prosecutor says, "We can't just take every case to court."

Right. Now, if it's a misdemeanor, because it doesn't involve an indictment, that's all done by the prosecutor. You can spend up to a year in jail just based on the prosecutor saying, "Here we go." That's an interesting pill to swallow.

8. Bail Process in Texas

Bail is an interesting concept. In most cases, if you're somebody who's never been accused or found guilty of a crime before, you're entitled to bond. Now, let's say capital murder was the issue. In that case, the state can make a move to deny you bail because our Texas constitution states that, under limited circumstances, you can be denied bail. For the other 99.9% of cases, though, you're entitled to bail. What the authority does then – be it the judge, the magistrate, the neutral magistrate, the city judge, some other official in the chain like a justice of the peace, or something like that – is set a bond amount. That bond amount then needs to be made, and it can be made a number of different ways. It can be made through pretrial services, which charges you a small percentage (sometimes as low as 3%) of the bond amount. It might also be a commercial bond based on the risk.

Now, the risk means a bondsman looks at it and says, "Okay. I trust this guy to come to court." He looks at the guy's criminal history and the nature of the charge, and then he says, "Okay. I'm going to set a risk at 10 to 15% of value of the bond." So then you pay him a fee up to that 10 to 15%, and it doesn't have to be paid all at one time normally, and then he gets some collateral for the full amount. So if you don't show up, he is allowed to move against the collateral. But you never get that 10 to 15% that you pay to the professional bondsman back. That's money based on the risk and the fee for the services provided.

In Texas, you are supposed to have that bond amount set within 24 hours of your arrest. Now, some law enforcement agencies will hold you incognito for up to 72 hours while they investigate the case. Once they charge you, though, you're to be seen by a magistrate within 24 hours to have bond set, and then off you go. Now, when the magistrate is looking to set bond, he is looking at the nature of the charge, the safety of the community, and the likelihood of that person showing back up balanced against that person's need to get out. He's trying to say, "Here is how much bond I think is reasonable to ensure that this individual will return to court." So he looks at them to see if they are a good person, if they have lived in the community for a while, if they have friends, family, and neighbors they are associated with, if they have been employed most of the time, and other things that keep them tied to the community no matter what the charge is. If it's somebody who's just passing through, they're probably not going to have a good bond.

If you've been in trouble many times before, you're also probably not going to have a good bond. We found that in 17.15 and 17.15(1) of the Texas Code of Criminal Procedure. Now, let's imagine that you've been convicted and the sentence has been suspended. We call that probation. Well, if that's happened, then you've been convicted of a crime. If you're then arrested on a revocation of that probation, you're not entitled to bond. The judges generally give it to you because they don't want you to sit in jail waiting for your case to proceed, which, if it's a felony, can sometimes take up to a couple of years based on the complexity of the case.

Can how busy the court's schedule is affect that as well?

Yes, absolutely. A lot of cases, though, just naturally take a long time. For instance, if it's a child abuse case, the first thing that happens is, if that child was accused of being abused by someone in the family — be it a father, a mother, or a step-parent — then that child is generally moved from one home to another for their own safety. Sometimes that home is out of state, and sometimes that child has to work to get acclimated to the new living environment, and to bring them back for this is sometimes traumatic. If they are in school and taking tests, then the schedule also becomes difficult. Tickets also have to be bought so far in advance because the State of Texas is complaining that they don't have the resources for it. Then the defense lawyer will have to get an expert to refute some of the accusations made by the state's expert. Sometimes it really is the complexity level of the case that can delay it while the evidence is being accumulated. Now, obviously a child who is involved in the case can come in and say this is what happened here. The defendant could then come back and say, "Well, that's not true." The prosecutor would want to bring in all the evidence they have, like medical records. Somebody has to explain all that, and it takes some time.

Now, in other cases involving violence, there might be text messages going back and forth or Facebook postings, and warrants have to be issued to out-of-state offices for Facebook, Myspace, or Twitter, which will then look at them. If they are a nation- or a worldwide organization, they will take that subpoena in the order they get it in, and they will give it their consideration, time, and effort, but we're not the only show in town. They could have literally hundreds ahead of this one. The same goes for phone records and financial records. Sometimes that's a difficulty.

I've seen cases where the evidence suddenly changed at the last second, and then we need a reset. So sometimes those delays are really caused not just by the court's availability but by the ability of the defendant or the State to get all the evidence they need to the courtroom.

When you talk about bond, are there bond conditions someone has to make sure they meet until they have to come to court?

There are a whole bunch of different conditions now. When you deal with domestic violence, sexual assault cases, or DWIs, the minimum conditions that you have to abide by are

right in our code of criminal procedure. For instance, you might not be allowed to go near school grounds or places where children congregate. Even though you're presumed innocent, it's just a precautionary measure. It's about the protection of the community.

Basically, what the judge wants to know is that you're not going to have contact with individuals who could be harmed. You're not going to be around your ex-spouse or this person you're alleged to have assaulted. Or if you came in and had all these controlled substances on you, then we want to take a urinalysis. We want to do these things to make sure that you're not getting in more trouble. We now have ankle monitors called SCRAM devices that analyze your sweat to determine if there is alcohol in it. If so, then you're going to have to come back to court and explain to the judge why you're drinking alcohol.

We have breathalyzers that are set up in homes so you'd have to periodically take a breath test in your home. Now, the defendants and the people on bond who are presumed innocent all pay for all this. Sometimes there are independent vendors who sell or lease these devices to the defendants, and they collect the money and issue report summaries to local probation officers who sometimes run the bond situation and/or local bond offices. The conditions are just designed to make sure somebody doesn't get in the same trouble again, and that they go out and get a job.

Sometimes if you have to have a bond hearing, it can take up to 10 to 14 days while you're in jail for it to get on the calendar and come to court. The arraignment process is only after you've waived indictment or have been indicted, and that could be 3 or 4 months down the road. Then you go for the arraignment, which is just to determine what you're charged with and if your name is spelled correctly, and just to make sure that we're talking about the same person and determine the identity. But your bond conditions are well ahead of anything else.

9. Pretrial Process in Texas

Once you are out of jail on bond, the rules for how often you go to court are really the same whether or not you're in jail. If you're out of jail, you have court dates and your lawyer shows up and you either accept or waive the arraignment. Again, if you want to be formally arraigned, then the prosecutor will read you the charge and you would enter an official plea of not guilty. If you waive arraignment, then you just sign a piece of paper saying, "Judge, I know what I am charged with, and yes, my name is Mr. A and that is who I am. It's spelled correctly in all manners and means."

After that, you'll have a pretrial, and that's really just a calendaring date where the judge wants to know 1) if you are ready, 2) if you have access to all the evidence, and 3) if you have had a chance to do an independent investigation with your lawyer to determine what has or has not happened. He also wants to know what you want to do with your case. Do you want to plead guilty? Do you want to have a non-jury trial? The judge then gives you a date that the trial will possibly occur.

Now, after that calendaring date, the number of times that you might have to go back to court really depends on you, your lawyer, and the complexity of the case. For instance, if it's the case that you believe that evidence was collected without proper authority, you can file a motion to suppress, which you would have to be there for. In testimony, an argument would be heard. In a criminal case of a certain level, every time the defendant's case is being presented, they must be there.

I've seen other cases where you go to a pretrial and then they come back with a plea to have it resolved. In other cases, we have a pretrial and then we're back there 4 to 5 times before the actual jury trial date because we're trying to narrow down the issues that we're in conflict with, such as evidence not taken permissibly or a test for the detection of an impaired driver that wasn't done correctly. Then we make our arguments to the judge and we try to have it kicked out because this wasn't done or this evidence isn't proper for a jury because it's not reliable. Really, you never know how many times you're going to go to court on a complex case.

10. Differences Between Felonies and Misdemeanors

The distinguishing factor between misdemeanors and felonies is the range of punishment. When you're dealing with misdemeanors, you could receive up to a year in jail (but not over) and, in Texas, up to a $4,000 fine. That one-year mark is the distinguishing feature. Now,

the legislature in each jurisdiction will determine which offenses are misdemeanors and which are felonies. For a felony offense, you can receive all the way up to the ultimate punishment, which is a death penalty. It's still a felony from a year in custody, though, with the possibility of going all the way up. For a misdemeanor, it's that year in custody all the way down that is the determining factor.

In Texas, we have many different levels of offenses. When you're dealing with a misdemeanor, we have a class C misdemeanor, which involves justice courts, municipal courts, speeding tickets, etc. You're not going into custody for those. Now, if you work out a fee payment arrangement and you fail to complete it, you can be arrested on a Capias pro fine charge to say that you need to pay. If you didn't show up at the court, you could be locked up for a little bit for failure to appear. On the actual charge itself, though, you cannot be confined.

Class B misdemeanors are punishable by up to 6 months in jail and up to a $3,000 fine. The majority of these cases are marijuana possession or a first-time DUI with under 0.15 on the blood alcohol test.

We then get up to the class A misdemeanors, and that's where you can get up to a year in jail and up to a $4,000 fine. A second or subsequent DUI with a blood alcohol level over 0.15, domestic violence, violence, soft tissue bodily injury — these are all examples.

Then we get into the felony range. We have the state jail felony, which means you can get sent to state jail for up to 2 years, or you can serve up to 180 days in the local county jail as a punishment. So the options are state jail from 180 days to 2 years, or under 180 days at a local community corrections facility, which in this case is our county jail.

You can have a third degree felony, which carries up to a $10,000 fine and up to 10 years in jail. Second-degree felonies carry up to a $10,000 fine and up to 20 years in jail. For a first-degree felony, you're looking at 5 to 99 years (or life), but you're still looking at a large range of punishment. If the sentence is 10 years or less, you're still eligible for probation. We also have "super felonies" for drugs, which means 15 to life and the probation is no longer an option, and that's where you just have a large quantity of drugs. Generally, if it's that much drugs, it would be dealt with in the federal system and states can't prosecute it.

Then we have what we call continuous sexual offenses, where it's 25 to life. We have the category of a subsequent offender, which means if somebody has a second felony offense, it kicks it up a grade. If it's a third, second, or first-degree felony or up, if you have a second offense, it bumps the punishment level up. If it's a first degree and you have a subsequent offense, then you're looking at 15 to life; for repeat offenders, 25 to life. Now, if you committed multiple or an earlier sex offense, and you have a second conviction on a similar charge, then you can get life imprisonment for that.

Now, life imprisonment is kind of hard to calculate because it's a real misnomer. What it generally means is anything above 60 years in confinement. Life just has a different component for getting out but you are still eligible for parole. Then we have capital murder, which carries a life sentence, and it’s 45 years before you're eligible for release. Finally, we have the possible death sentence.

So we have many different types of penalties in our penal code and our code of criminal procedure. We also have a number of different codes that have offenses that aren't articulated what penalty they carry; those have their own offense schedule. But just dealing with our local codes, that is the punishment range and the types of felonies and misdemeanors we have.

How often are you able to get charges dropped or at least reduced?

Really, it happens a lot, because every case is different. When you're dealing with different prosecutors, you're dealing with different individuals. When you're dealing with misdemeanors, it's particularly common, because their goal there is not to just punish; their goal is mainly to make sure that this conduct, if it is criminal conduct, doesn't happen again. You also have the ability to talk to people or to set the case for trial and look at the facts of the case and the investigation. There are all kinds of different ways to do it but it happens.

Now, if somebody's been in trouble multiple times, that's really not going to happen as easily. It could happen, but it's not going to be an easy thing to do. You just have to do a thoughtful, complete, comprehensive, and thorough investigation, and review the police's investigation. In these cases, you're looking for areas where you can have a meeting of the minds about something not being fair or a charge being inappropriate. Sometimes it even works to go in and say, "You know what? If you dismiss this case, you're never going to see this person again, because this is once-in-a-lifetime thing. They're not going to come back."

Now sometimes we do agree to pay a larger fine for less possible time in custody or else less time on probation because it might not be nearly as difficult as paying the money. That’s our way of saying, "We won't be back. This is an investment for him to show you he won't be in trouble again."

11. Alternative Punishments for Crimes Committed in Texas

We have many different options. A lot of those options obviously have to have the prosecutor's understanding and consent in some courts. Remember, each county runs its courts differently, be it a prostitution court, a drug court, or a veteran's court. The eligibility is not set statewide; it's set by each county and is based on whether that county feels it fit to administer that program.

For instance, we have a mental health docket, which is designed to bring medical providers or mental health providers to the courthouse so they can interact with people who are accused of crimes because of some difficulties in their lives. As an example, you would see homeless people who have a mental illness and who are continuously charged with criminal trespassing because they're on the storefront. They can go to the local convenience store, the 7-Eleven, the Costco, and the lawyer, and they can get arrested for criminal trespassing because they've been warned. These are the kinds of cases specialty courts deal with.

Now, in our system, we rarely deal with house arrest. Probation is where you're sentenced to some type of confinement and they suspend the sentence. Deferred adjudication is a little bit different in that you've never been found guilty; that's very important for work, licenses, and programs. No one ever wants to be convicted because it has a wide range of effects; you can even lose your ability to vote. So it's very important that there are those programs.

Diversion programs are based on individual counties. Bell County and the adjacent counties have diversion programs where you are really monitored by a probation officer or by the prosecutor's office for compliance. If you do well, they never file charges. You sign a contract with them that states that you are going to do X, Y, and Z, and in return for that, you never go to court.

Community service is mandatory in Texas, particularly for criminal cases, unless there is a good reason why not. These reasons vary, but generally it's a case-by-case thing. Really, everything is possible, except for the house arrest. Everything else, though? Absolutely. There is a whole bunch of alternatives.

12. Reasons You Should Hire an Experienced Attorney to Defend Your Case

Well, there are many reasons. First of all, you never want to go to talk to the police by yourself because you don't know what the facts are that are important. The attorney will be able to see if there is not reliable evidence or if the officer did the investigation incorrectly on this occasion. You're looking for somebody who is going to recognize what's important. A lot of the time when we're sick, we diagnose ourselves as having a cold or fever. When it continues, though, we go to the doctor. The difference here is that you don't know if it's gotten worse when you're talking to law enforcement and the prosecutor. By the time you go talk to your lawyer, that time has come and gone. You've given a statement or you've said something.

Public defenders have a bad rap. There are a lot of misconceptions when it comes to them, so people want to hire their own lawyer. Really, though, when you deal with public defenders, you are dealing with people who are taking every case that comes in. What that means is that the court will appoint them. If they are court-appointed attorneys or if they work for a public defender's office, then whatever case comes in, they are going to be assigned to it. It could be a DWI, it could be possession of a controlled substance, it could be homicide, or it could be a sexual assault case. Just because they're qualified to handle the case doesn't make them an expert.

When you meet a lawyer, your questions need to be: How many cases do you have right now? What's your caseload like? How much time do you have to do an independent investigation? What you're trying to find out is not necessarily if he has free time but how he's going to spend his time representing you. What type of time does he have? What are his commitments? What kinds of complications does the case have? Is this a type of case he's handled many times before? How many DWIs have you dealt with? How many of those involved the Intoxilyzer 9000? Since I first started, we've had around 5,000. How many cases have you handled involving a blood draw? How many of them have you been involved with that have had a blood draw and a location other than a hospital or an EMS facility? You want to ask questions, and of course you want to have your own attorney be able to talk to you, get back to you for a few moments, and give you all the time you need. You want to be able to schedule an appointment and come in, and for the lawyer to give you what you've paid for.

Public defenders and court-appointed lawyers have a lot of cases to handle — so much, in fact, that the State of Texas now requires lawyers who work on a court-appointed basis to state how many cases they handle in general, their total number of cases, and how many of those are court-appointed.

Why should they come to me? I'm board-certified in criminal law and have been since 1996. I have been a prosecutor, I have been in private practice, and I've literally represented or prosecuted every type of case all the way down to a speeding ticket or a minor possession, as well as litigations. I was also a municipal prosecutor and a municipal judge, so I've seen from all different sides how these things work and how they are going to apply to you based on my experience and based on the time I'm going to spend learning about your case. I can tailor your defense and your representation in such a way that it's going to ensure that we get the best possible outcome. When I say "ensure," I mean that we can do everything possible.

Do you have any favorite stories or victories from among the cases that you've defended over the years?

There've just been so many cases, and the ones that we get a successful outcome on are just always special in and of themselves. Everyone that we've gotten a good outcome for really always stands out. The people stand out, and their hopes and dreams and fears stand out, and so I'd like to say that there've been so many favorite cases.

I've dealt with kids who were accused of sexual assault and they had some mental problems and found out that they were the scapegoat. Now, what happened was that the individual, a young girl, didn't want to admit that she was having a relationship with a neighbor who was much older, so they found the mentally handicapped individual and decided to pick on him. It took well over 2 years to exonerate, but in those 2 years, he didn't participate in any extracurricular activities and he was shunned by all of the people he went to school with. It was such a great ending but it was devastating for him.

I've had a child accused of having sex with a girl when he was much older, but he was mentally challenged. So who was really the victim in that case? It took us years to resolve that case. And still the stigma applies, even though he wasn't guilty because he didn't know what he was doing. This was a very difficult type of case where people spent literally years in jail but the jury acquitted them in less than 10 minutes. We were excited by it, but at the same time, he was in custody all that time because every dollar they had went towards his attorney and his investigator to bring that evidence to court. His life was ruined. It was devastating. It's always so difficult to determine what is a win and what is a loss. For me, the win is a favorable outcome, even though that can still be a loss to the accused because their life has been turned upside down. So I don't know. I just don't think I have a favorite anymore.

Sometimes, we're up in the front of the courtroom laughing and joking with the prosecutors because we know each other, or I'm asking them about their day because of the things we have in common, or we see them in the local community. The prosecutors are still looking for signs of weakness and strength, though – weakness in your clients and how your client knew how to react in court because you spent time with them. You take them into the courtroom before they are supposed to get there, you look at it, and you show them where everybody stands. You say, "They are going to call your name and you are going to stand up. I'm going to stand up. I'm going to look right at the judge. If the judge says this man is not guilty, then we need a trial or a trial by jury or something of that nature." When the prosecutor turns around and looks at the defendant, they are looking at them to see if they are ready to fold, and you can't let that happen because that's what the prosecutor's hoping for. What really sets us apart is that we cover every facet of this and we leave nothing to chance to be misunderstood. We will show them the pictures of the judges, so that when they are walking down the hallway or are —heaven forbid – in the bathroom, they don't say something stupid with the judge standing next to them. All these things are important. You also never cut anybody off on the way to the courthouse. That could be one of the jurors.

Anything could happen at the courthouse, so we don't want to leave anything to chance. The reason why our clients pay us is 1) they've never been through the process, and 2) they haven't gone through the process with somebody they felt comfortable enough with to go back to for the next go-around.

There are times when you need to put your faith in somebody else, and that's what we're here for. It's to say that we are that "somebody else" and that this is the right choice and also to ensure them. When somebody hires us, I tell them that immediately, because I know they are concerned about whether they made the right choice in coming to me, and because they need to know that they are doing the right thing for their future right then and there.

Made in the USA
Monee, IL
05 November 2026

67385059R00033